Printed in the United States of America

First Printing, 2013

ISBN-13: 978-1489522214
ISBN-10: 1489522212
www.aisforarray.com

A is for array

Written by Brandon Hansen

Designed & Illustrated by Ben Coleman & Lucas Hogg

Autumn, Benjamin, and Clay, I am proud of who you are. I am proud of your curiosity and growth. Whatever you set your mind to, you will succeed in. I wrote this book for you guys. Someday, you too will eat candy and play on your computer. I love you kids! And Melissa, thank you for putting up with me constantly trying to explain code to you. I love you forever.

A is for array

A place to store your toy collection.

Just as a toy box keeps your toys together, and a tool box keeps my tools in one place, an array is used by programs to make it much easier to find related information.

B is for boolean

Either on or off.
Like a light or the TV.

Sometimes we ask, "what do you want to do today?" Other times we ask, "did you have fun?" and you say, "yes" or "no". Programmers use booleans when they just need the simple yes or no.

C is for constructor

Get together a blanket and chairs. It's fort time!

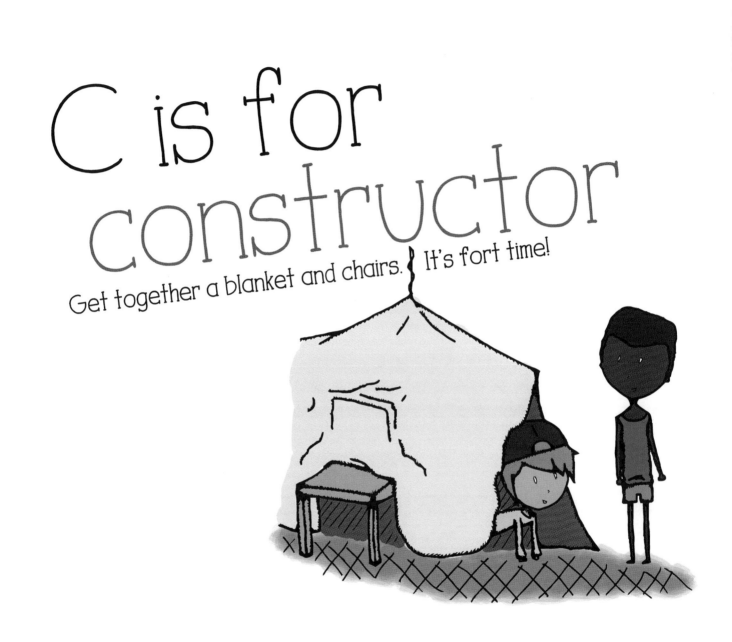

When you create a fort, you first have to get the blanket and chairs together.   Constructors in programming help get everything together. Now you can start building.

D is for DeConstructor

Let your mom clean up after you. That's her job.

Once you are done building, you have to tear it all down, otherwise the program will get all messy and could come crashing down. That is what a deconstructor helps you do. Oh, just kidding about your mom having to clean up after you. That is your job, silly!

E is for explode

How many bumps are on an egg?
Let's find out!

Sometimes a program needs to know how many words are in a sentence or how many sentences are in a book. Explode (or split) lets us separate the words so we can count them.

F is for function

Taking a picture is a function of your camera

A function is a block of code used to divide code up so it can be reused across the program and even sometimes in other programs. With a function, we can tell our camera "take a picture", and let it do all the work.

G is for global

Cookies: loved by children around the world.

Cookies

No matter where you go, no matter who you are, you breathe air, and drink water. Without access to air and water, humans cannot exist. Some programs have their own functions that they need to be able to access everywhere. Those are called globals.

H is for heap

Clean clothes go here.
Dirty clothes go there.

Just as we sort lights and darks (sometimes) when we are doing laundry, we also sort data in our programs to make certain tasks more easy to perform.

I is for
inheritance

You got your momma's eyes!

Just like you have some features that your mom has, code can inherit qualities from other code. And just as you have your own qualities, code that inherits can be given its own properties.

J is for join

We are all one family!

When we are playing with toys, sometimes you say, "can I have my baby AND my puppy?" In our programs we often need to look up information in different categories at the same time. Joins get us everything that we are looking for.

K is for key

Like your fingerprint,
everyone is unique.

The police use fingerprints to help them find people. That is because each person has their own fingerprints. It is similar in programming. We can often find what we are looking for because we use a unique key to store our information.

L is for loop

Duck, duck, goose!

Keep going until you get to goose!

Just like you keep saying, "duck" until you get to a goose, programs go in loops until they find what they are looking for. Sometimes they never find it and they go forever.

M is for mutable

Playdough can change shape and color.

Playdough allows you to shape it and mold it. Sometimes you even mix it and create new colors. But you can't shape or mold your shoes. Once they are created they will be the same forever. It is that way in code, too. Some code lets you change it after you make it. Some code stays the same forever.

N is for namespace

A name helps people know who you are.

Some programs get really big. A namespace is a tool that helps us to organize so we don't get confused about what code we are using. It is just like how you have a first, middle, and last name. If there is someone with the same first name as you, we can call you by your full name.

O is for object

Your cat, your dog and all your toys are all objects.

Just like how you can tell it is a dog because it barks, has a tail, and four legs, programmers create objects in their code that have certain traits. Programs are, as often as possible, modeled after the real world.

P is for persistence

Like writing a journal.
It will be remembered forever.

Whenever we go on trips, or have birthday parties, we take pictures and put them in the scrap book. But then sometimes our memories are just in our heads. Programs do the same thing. Some information gets stored forever. Some information is only temporary.

Q is for query

Need to find a word?
Use a dictionary to find it!

Back when I was a kid I used to go and look things up in a book called the dictionary. I would say, "tell me what the word 'silly' means" and it would tell me. Programs look up information in a very similar way, and that is referred to as a query.

R is for recursion

Trees have seeds that make new trees.

Much like a sunflower or a tree have seeds in them that fall and create new trees, code can execute itself. This is called recursion, and is often seen in mathematical programs.

S is for singleton

There is only one you!

No matter how many times I say your name, I am still referring to the same you. But it isn't that way in most code. Most of the time programs create a new object every time you call them. Singletons, however, use the same object over and over.

T is for try/catch

Climb that tree! Don't worry, we have bandages to fix you!

When you make a mistake, sometimes we can clean up the mess and make sure that everything is fixed up. Sometimes bad things happen in code. When we use try/catch we can try to clean up a bit and maybe even try again.

U is for
undefined

Just like the boogey-man, it doesn't exist.

There is nothing scary in your closet or under your bed. But I will always check for you just to make sure. Every once in a while we have to do that in our code, too. Even though we are pretty sure that an object doesn't exist, we still have to check to make sure. If it isn't there, it is called undefined.

V is for variable

Is it rainy? Sunny?

The weather is a variable.

A progam uses variables to hold some information. This is just like how you might say, "the weather is sunny" or "the weather is rainy". Variables let us make decisions in our program. If the weather is rainy, we might show an umbrella on the screen.

W is for while

While there is food on your plate, you will sit there.

While is just another type of loop that programs use. Instead of saying, "get me when I get to goose", you might say, "hold still while I am still saying duck."

X is for XP

Try, try again. Keep building your fort until you get it right!

Programmers used to spend years trying to create the perfect program, having meetings with lots of important people, and missing deadlines. Often when people could finally buy the program, it wasn't as good as it could be. So some smart people said, "maybe we should do it different." Let's put out chairs, then find a blanket big enough. If we like it, then we are done. If not, let's make it bigger and better.

Y is for YAML

Momma keeps her
shopping list in YAML

Ice Cream, Berries, Apples, Pizza. Oh my. We could wander all over the store for hours! So some people made it really easy to organize information. They called it YAML. Now we can store our shopping list like this:

```
food:
  frozen: ice cream
  fresh: berries, apples
  baked: pizza, bread
```

See, much better! That should save us some time!

Z is for
Z-Index

It's a dog pile! The one
on top is the biggest Z!

The world around you is filled with shapes. Buildings reaching the sky, birds sitting on the rooftops, and airplanes soaring through the sky. Computers screens, though, are flat. But that is no good. So we needed a way to make things look real and stack them on top of each other. That is the magic of the z-index.

The End

Made in the USA
Lexington, KY
27 April 2014